BRANCH LINES TO PRINCES RISBOROUGH

Vic Mitchell and Keith Smith

Cover picture: A typical branch train was recorded from the down platform at Princes Risborough on 26th July 1947. No. 1426 is coupled to autocoach no. 81, a type of formation that could be seen on all three routes. (H.C.Casserley)

Published April 2003

ISBN 1 904474 05 5

© Middleton Press, 2003

Design   Deborah Esher
            David Pede
Typesetting Barbara Mitchell

Published by
            Middleton Press
            Easebourne Lane
            Midhurst, West Sussex
            GU29 9AZ
Tel: 01730 813169
Fax: 01730 812601
Email: enquiries@middletonpress.fsnet.co.uk

Printed & bound by Biddles Ltd,
            Guildford and Kings Lynn

CONTENTS

1.	From Aylesbury	1-20	3.	From Watlington	73-108
2.	From Oxford	21-72	4.	Princes Risborough	109-120

INDEX

28	Abingdon Road Halt	15	Little Kimble	13	South Aylesbury Halt
85	Aston Rowant	33	Littlemore	49	Tiddington
1	Aylesbury	29	Kennington Junction	54	Thame
67	Bledlow	91	Kingston Crossing Halt	64	Towersey Halt
105	Bledlow Bridge Halt	18	Monks Risborough	104	Wainhill Crossing Halt
93	Chinnor	36	Morris Cowley	73	Watlington
42	Horspath Halt	21	Oxford	44	Wheatley
83	Lewknor Bridge Halt	109	Princes Risborough		

I. Map of the Wycombe Railway with additions up to 1933. (Railway Magazine)

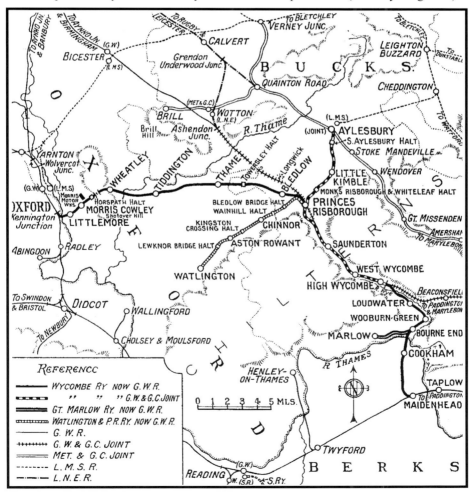

ACKNOWLEDGEMENTS

Our sincere gratitude goes to so many of the photographers who have helped us and also to W.R.Burton, the BMW Press Office, L.Crosier, G.Croughton, F.Hornby, N.Langridge, S.C.Nash, Mr D. and Dr S.Salter, J.Tremaine, E.Youldon and, as always, our wives.

GEOGRAPHICAL SETTING

Princes Risborough and the Watlington branch lie at the foot of the scarp edge of the Chiltern Hills, their Chalk providing the raw material for cement production at Chinnor.

The River Thame flows from the area north of the market centre of Aylesbury, close to the town of Thame and into the Thames north-east of Didcot. The Thame-Oxford line passes over the River Thame east of Wheatley and then climbs over a ridge of high ground which includes outcrops of Portland Beds. It descends into the Thames Valley south of Oxford. All three routes pass over Upper Greensand and Gault Clay in their first two or three miles after leaving Princes Risborough.

The lines were in Buckinghamshire and Oxfordshire, the boundary being shown with dots on map I.

The maps are to the scale of 25ins to 1 mile, unless otherwise stated. North is at the top, except where indicated by an arrow.

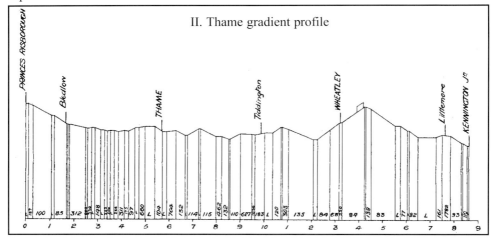

II. Thame gradient profile

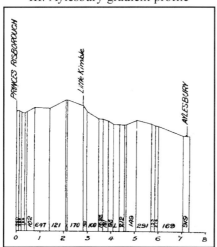

III. Aylesbury gradient profile

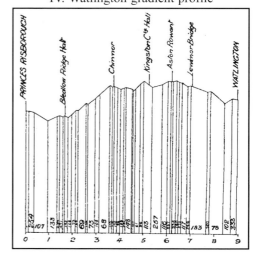

IV. Watlington gradient profile

HISTORICAL BACKGROUND

The single broad gauge track Wycombe Railway was extended from High Wycombe to Thame on 1st August 1862 and it opened a branch from Princes Risborough to Aylesbury on 1st October 1863. The Thame-Oxford section first saw trains on 24th October 1864, the line joining the 1844 branch from Didcot at Kennington Junction.

These lines became part of the Great Western Railway in 1867 and were converted to standard gauge in 1868 (to Aylesbury) and 1870 (Thame route).

The Watlington & Princes Risborough Railway's Act of Parliament on 26th July 1869 authorised a light railway between these places and its opening took place on 15th August 1872. It was acquired by the GWR on 1st July 1883, the stock including two locomotives.

The Metropolitan Railway extended its route from London to reach Aylesbury in 1892 and the Great Central Railway arrived from the north in 1899 using the 1868 Buckingham & Aylesbury Railway. The first line to the town had been the 1839 branch from the London & Birmingham Railway. The GCR arranged to run over the MR into London, but, finding this unsatisfactory, made an agreement with the GWR for a joint route via Princes Risborough and High Wycombe.

The first part of the direct line from Princes Risborough to Banbury opened in 1905. This section was operated jointly by the GWR and GCR.

All the routes described herein became part of the Western Region of British Railways upon nationalisation in 1948 and remained single track. The Watlington branch lost its passenger service on 1st July 1957 and passenger trains on the Thame route ended on 7th January 1963. Freight withdrawal dates are given in the captions.

The Aylesbury branch was in the London Midland Region from 1958 to 1973, but was back in the Western Region until becoming part of Network SouthEast in 1986. Following privatisation on 21st July 1996, services have been provided by Chiltern Railways, the operating name of M40 Trains Ltd.

The Chinnor & Princes Risborough Railway revived the northern part of the Watlington branch between those places during the 1990s, but was not able to gain access to the latter station. It was a case of history repeating itself, as the WPRR had the same problem from 1872 to 1883.

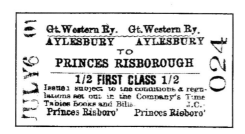

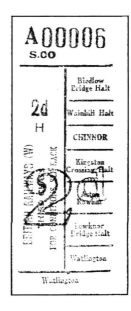

PASSENGER SERVICES

To Aylesbury

The tables in this section indicate down train frequency in selected years and include only those running on at least five days per week. The one below shows how greatly the service has fluctuated, a notable increase coming around 1905 when the main line south of Princes Risborough was doubled. The main reduction took place in the early 1960s, when that route was down graded and dieselisation took place.

	Weekdays	Sundays
1869	3	0
1892	6	2
1913	13	3
1932	15	6
1952	15	3
1972	7	1
1992	9	0
2002	26	10

To Thame and Oxford

	Weekdays	Sundays
1869	4	3
1892	6	2
1913	6	2
1932	5	2
1952	8	2
1963	5	2

There were additional trains from Princes Risborough to Thame on weekdays. The 1932 timetable showed three, 1952 eight and 1963 five. There were some extra trains for car workers at Morris Cowley; these are mentioned in caption 36, but they terminated there for a few years only.

To Watlington

	Weekdays	Sundays
1873	3	?
1882	3	2
1892	3	?
1913	6	0
1932	6	0
1952	5	0
1956	5	0

Some early timetables were ambiguous about Sunday services. They ran for many other years, but officially carried milk only. There was an additional journey on a Wednesday and/or a Saturday shown in many early timetables.

July 1913

April 1932

LONDON, PRINCES RISBOROUGH, THAME and OXFORD

Miles		Week Days															Sundays			
		am	am		am		pm S	pm		pm E	pm E		pm S	pm S	pm E	pm S	am		pm	
	57 London (M'lebone) A dep	6 55	..	..	10 20	..	1 20	2 20	..	3 40	5 33	..	5 20	..	6 33	7 20	9 35	..	..	..
	57 „ (Pad.) A „	..	9 10	..	..	..	..	..	..	4 15	..	..	..	..	..	..	9 30	..	6 10	..
		②	②				②	②		②	②		②	②	②	②	②		②	
—	**Princes Risborough** dep	8 24	10 7	..	11 33	..	2 38	4 4	..	5 44	6 48	..	6 48	..	8 10	8 32	11 5	..	7 20	..
1½	Bledlow	8 28	10 11	..	11 37	..	2 42	4 8	..	5 48	6 52	..	6 52	..	8 14	8 36	11 9	..	7 24	..
4½	Towersey Halt	8 33	10 16	..	11 42	..	2 47	4 13	..	5 53	6 57	..	6 57	..	8 19	8 41	11 14	..	7 29	..
5¾	Thame	8 38	10 22	..	11 45	..	2 52	4 17	..	6 0	7 1	..	7 1	..	8 23	8 45	11K22	..	7 33	..
9¾	Tiddington	8 46	10 30	..	..	..	3 0	4 25	..	6 8	7 9	..	7 9	..	8 31	8 53	11 30	..	7 41	..
13¼	Wheatley	8 53	10 38	..	..	..	3 12	4 32	..	6 14	7 21	..	7 15	7 32	8 38	9 0	11 39	..	7 48	..
15	Horspath Halt	8 58	10 43	..	..	..	3 17	4 37	..	..	7 26	..	..	7 37	8 43	9 5	11 44	..	7 53	..
16¼	Morris Cowley	9 3	10 47	..	..	..	3 21	4 41	..	..	7 31	..	..	7 43	8 47	9 9	..	..	..	..
17½	Littlemore	9 7	10 51	..	..	..	3 25	4 45	..	..	7 35	..	..	7 47	8 51	9 13	11 52	..	8 0	..
21	**Oxford** arr	9 15	10 58	..	..	..	3 32	4 52	..	..	7 43	..	..	7 55	8 58	9 20	12 0	..	8 8	..
84½	61 London (Pad.) A.. arr	11 0	12 28	..	..	..	5 39	6G38	..	..	10 0	..	..	10 0	11 39	11 39	2J58	..	10 5	..

Miles		Week Days																Sundays			
		am W	am	am		pm		am S	pm		pm		pm E		pm			am		pm	
	61 London (Pad.) A.. dep	..	5 30	..	..	..	..	11 15	1 15	..	3 15	..	..	..	5 15	..	..	..	..	..	..
			②	②				②	②		②		②		②			②		②	
—	**Oxford** dep	6 49	7 50	..	..	..	..	1 20	2 47	..	4 45	..	..	..	6 50	..	..	10 0	..	5 50	..
3½	Littlemore	6 56	7 58	..	..	..	..	1 28	2 55	..	4 53	..	..	..	6 58	..	..	10 8	..	5 58	..
4¾	Morris Cowley	7B10	8 3	..	..	..	..	1 33	3 0	..	4 58	..	..	..	7 3	..	..	..	..	..	..
6	Horspath Halt	7 15	8 8	..	..	..	..	1 38	3 5	..	5 3	..	..	..	7 8	..	..	10 16	..	6 6	..
7¾	Wheatley	7 22	8 14	..	..	..	..	1 44	3 10	..	5 8	..	..	..	7 16	..	..	10 22	..	6 13	..
11¼	Tiddington	7 30	8 21	..	..	..	..	1 51	3 17	..	5 15	..	..	..	7 23	..	..	10 29	..	6 21	..
15¼	Thame	7C45	8 28	3 51	..	12 19	..	1 59	3 25	..	5 23	..	6 15	..	7 31	..	..	10 38	..	6K33	..
16½	Towersey Halt	7 49	Z	8 55	..	12 23	..	2 3	3 29	..	5 27	..	6 19	..	7 35	..	..	10 42	..	6 37	..
19½	Bledlow	7 56	..	9 2	..	12 30	..	2 10	3 36	..	5 34	..	6 26	..	7 42	..	..	10 49	..	6 44	..
21	**Princes Risborough** arr	8 0	..	9 6	..	12 34	..	2 14	3 40	..	5 38	..	6 30	..	7 46	..	..	10 53	..	6 48	..
55¾	57 London (Pad.) A.. arr	..	..	10 4	..	1 36	..	..	..	..	..	..	8 17	..	..	..	..	..	..	..	..
57	57 „ (M'lebone) A „	9H14	..	..	..	..	..	3 58	4 58	..	6S58	..	..	..	9L28	..	..	12 13	..	8 13	..

A First and Second class
B Arr 10 minutes *earlier*
C Arr 8 minutes *earlier*
E Except Saturdays
G Arr 6 50 pm on Saturdays
H On Saturdays arr 9 33 am
J Until 21st October inclusive, 16th, 23rd and 30th December, 1962 and commencing 31st March, 1963 arr 2 40 pm
K Arr 5 minutes *earlier*
L On Saturdays arr 8 58 pm
S Saturdays only
W Through train from Banbury (dep 5 55 am) to Princes Risborough (Table 152). Second class only
Z For continuation, see next column
② Second class only

September 1963

April 1932

LONDON, PRINCES RISBORO' and WATLINGTON (Rail Auto Cars—One Class only).

Miles	Down.	Week Days only.						Sats. only.
		C	mrn	aft	aft	aft	aft	aft
	42 London (Pad.) ..dep.	5 45	9 10	1225	2 23	4 40	7A10	9 0
—	Princes Risboro' ¶..dep.	8B3	10 6	1 55	3 55	5 45	7 57	1055
3¾	Chinnor	8B12	1019	2 6	4 6	5 56	8 8	11 6
6¾	Aston Rowant	8B18	1029	2 13	4 13	6 3	8 15	1113
9	Watlington ¶ ......arr.	8B25	1036	2 21	4 21	6 11	8 23	1121

Miles	Up.	Week Days only.					
		C	mrn	mrn	aft	aft	aft
	Watlington ¶..........dep.	7 30	8 40	1130	2 58	4 33	6 50
2¾	Aston Rowant	7 38	8 50	1138	3 6	4 41	7 0
5¼	Chinnor..........[98. 844	7 45	8 58	1145	3 13	4 48	7 10
9	Princes Risboro' ¶ 43, arr.	7 56	9 10	1156	3 24	4 59	7 21
43¾	43 London (Paddington) arr.	9 19	10 0	1 40	4 38	6 40	9 20

A Slip Carriage. B Not calling at the Halts. C Mons. only.
¶ "Halts" at Bledlow Bridge and at Wainhill, between Princes Risboro' and Chinnor; at Kingston Crossing between Chinnor and Aston Rowant; and at Lewknor Bridge, between Aston Rowant and Watlington.

September 1956

LONDON, PRINCES RISBOROUGH and WATLINGTON
(Second class only, except where otherwise shown)
WEEK DAYS ONLY

Miles		am				pm S				pm				pm						pm	
	57 London (M'lebone) dep	..	..	..	..	..	..	..	..	12K20	..	..	..	4H10	..	..	..	..	..	6 50	..
	57 „ (Pad.) A „	9H10	..	..	..	..	..	..	..	..	..	..	..	4 34	..	..	..	..	..	..	..
—	**Princes Risborough**...dep	10 22	..	..	..	12 20	..	..	..	2 5	..	..	..	5 48	..	..	..	..	..	8 20	..
1¾	Bledlow Bridge Halt	10 27	..	..	..	12 25	..	..	..	2 10	..	..	..	5 53	..	..	..	..	..	8 25	..
3	Wainhill Halt	10 30	..	..	..	12 28	..	..	..	2 13	..	..	..	5 56	..	..	..	..	..	8 28	..
3¾	Chinnor	10 33	..	..	..	12 31	..	..	..	2 16	..	..	..	5 59	..	..	..	..	..	8 31	..
5¼	Kingston Crossing Halt	10 42	..	..	..	12 40	..	..	..	2 25	..	..	..	6 8	..	..	..	..	..	8 40	..
6¾	Aston Rowant	10 49	..	..	..	12 47	..	..	..	2 32	..	..	..	6 15	..	..	..	..	..	8 47	..
7	Lewknor Bridge Halt	10 55	..	..	..	12 53	..	..	..	2 38	..	..	..	6 21	..	..	..	..	..	8 53	..
9	**Watlington** arr	11 7	..	..	..	1 5	..	..	..	2 50	..	..	..	6 33	..	..	..	..	..	9 5	..
Mls		am				am				am				pm S				pm			pm
—	**Watlington** dep	7 0	..	..	..	8 30	..	..	..	11 20	..	..	..	1 12	..	..	..	3 0	..	..	7 15
2	Lewknor Bridge Halt	7 12	..	..	..	8 42	..	..	..	11 32	..	..	..	1 24	..	..	..	3 12	..	..	7 27
2¾	Aston Rowant	7 18	..	..	..	8 48	..	..	..	11 38	..	..	..	1 30	..	..	..	3 18	..	..	7 33
3¾	Kingston Crossing Halt	7 25	..	..	..	8 55	..	..	..	11 45	..	..	..	1 37	..	..	..	3 25	..	..	7 40
5¼	Chinnor	7 34	..	..	..	9 4	..	..	..	11 54	..	..	..	1 46	..	..	..	3 34	..	..	7 49
6	Wainhill Halt	7 37	..	..	..	9 7	..	..	..	11 57	..	..	..	1 49	..	..	..	3 37	..	..	7 52
7¼	Bledlow Bridge Halt	7 40	..	..	..	9 10	..	..	..	12 0	..	..	..	1 52	..	..	..	3 40	..	..	7 55
9	**Princes Risborough.** arr	7 45	..	..	..	9 15	..	..	..	12 5	..	..	..	1 57	..	..	..	3 45	..	..	8 0
43¾	57 London (Pad.) A . arr	9G34	..	..	..	10 10	..	..	..	1 32	..	..	..	..	..	..	..	..	..	..	..
45	57 „ (M'lebone) „	9E17	..	..	..	..	..	..	..	..	..	..	..	3 8	..	..	..	5H 3	..	..	10 4

A First and Second class
E Except Saturdays
G Via Maidenhead. Arr Paddington 9 36 am on Saturdays
H Change at High Wycombe
K On Mondays to Fridays change at High Wycombe
S Saturdays only

1. From Aylesbury

AYLESBURY

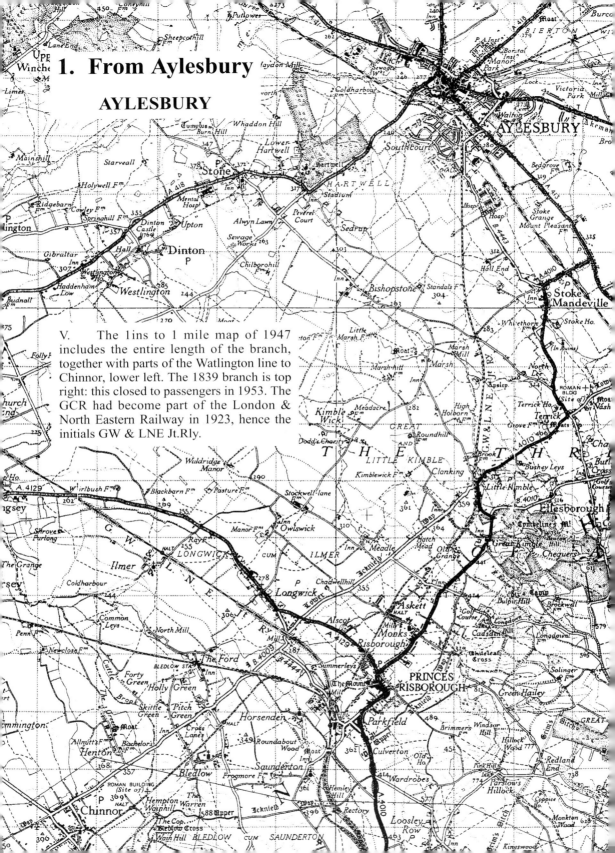

V. The 1ins to 1 mile map of 1947 includes the entire length of the branch, together with parts of the Watlington line to Chinnor, lower left. The 1839 branch is top right: this closed to passengers in 1953. The GCR had become part of the London & North Eastern Railway in 1923, hence the initials GW & LNE Jt.Rly.

1. A single wooden platform served until 1st January 1894 when the Metropolitan Railway ceased to use its temporary terminus east of the junction with the GWR branch. The three platforms of the joint station came into use at that time. This southward view is from 1908 and includes two signal boxes. The one on the left was about to be demolished following the elimination of reverse curves on which an express had derailed in 1904. (Lens of Sutton coll.)

2. The platforms were all lengthened in 1926; this one had ended near the open door until that time. No. 2222 is seen with the 12.5pm departure for Paddington on 15th March 1930, alongside a grounded Metropolitan Railway coach. (H.C.Casserley)

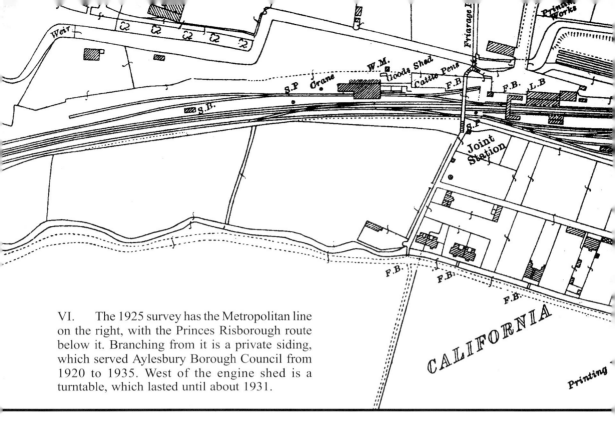

VI. The 1925 survey has the Metropolitan line on the right, with the Princes Risborough route below it. Branching from it is a private siding, which served Aylesbury Borough Council from 1920 to 1935. West of the engine shed is a turntable, which lasted until about 1931.

3. The Joint station was built in 1893 and its entrance was recorded in the 1960s. The end of the bay platform is in shadow on the left. On the right are Morris vans of the Royal Mail. The suffix "Town" was applied officially from 25th September 1950 until 2nd December 1963, but revisions to signs took place sometime after. (J.Scott-Morgan coll.)

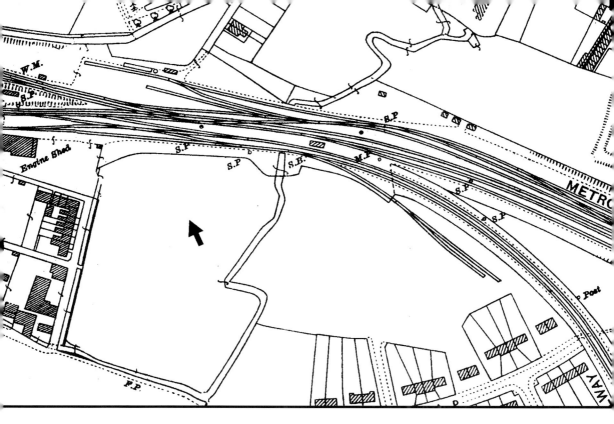

4.   The goods shed is visible below the footbridge; freight service was withdrawn on 2nd December 1974. BR class 2-6-0 no. 76043 stands near the ex-GWR engine shed, which had been a sub-shed of Slough (81B) before transfer to Bletchley (4A) and then to Neasden (14D) in 1958. (Lens of Sutton coll.)

5. Ex-GCR class N5 0-6-2T no. 69273 arrives with the 3.5pm empty stock from Princes Risborough on 22nd April 1953. The Eastern Region train worked the morning service on the branch. (N.W.Sprinks)

6. Sister engine no. 69369 approaches the station with the afternoon freight from Princes Risborough on 6th May 1953. More wagons stand in the 1900 sidings in the background. The LNER provided station staff from 1923 to 1948. (N.W.Sprinks)

7. This bay platform was added on the north side of the station in 1926. It is seen in the 1960s and was eliminated in November 1990. The dock on the right had cattle pens in earlier times. (Lens of Sutton coll.)

8. The Chilterns are in the background in this panorama from 17th May 1962. The rear of the 6.25pm to Maidenhead is featured, while near it is 2-6-4T no. 42090. On the coal road is 2-6-2T no. 84029. The final GWR allocation in 1947 was one 2-6-2T and one 0-4-2T. (B.Jennings)

9. The ornate part of the coal stage had once supported a water tank. Seen with autocoach *Thrush* is 0-4-2T no. 1440 taking water on 16th June 1962, prior to working all stations to High Wycombe. This was the last day of autotrain working and life at this shed. (B.Jennings)

10. North Box closed in 1967 and Aylesbury South lost its suffix at that time. It is seen on 4th October 1990 as preparations were being made for its demise on 3rd December following. DMUs arrive from Marylebone, left, and Princes Risborough, right. (M.J.Stretton)

11. Taken from the same point on the footbridge as picture no. 8, this view features no. 5029 *Nunney Castle*, which was attending an event which involved five steam trips to Princes Risborough, but not to Cornwall. The new diesel depot was the centre of the Aylesbury Gala Day on 25th April 1992. (P.G.Barnes)

12. A DMU maintenance depot was built north of the station in 1991 for the new fleet of class 165 units. The depot was transferred from Chiltern Railways to ADtranz on 15th September 1996. (M.Turvey)

SOUTH AYLESBURY HALT

13. The halt opened on 13th February 1933 and served some new factories and housing. It was situated on the B4443 and generated little traffic. Oil lamps in an urban area were somewhat incongruous. (Lens of Sutton coll.)

14. The 6.25pm Aylesbury to Maidenhead usually had three coaches, five vans and about the same number of passengers. It is seen in May 1962; the halt closed on 5th June 1967. (B.Jennings)

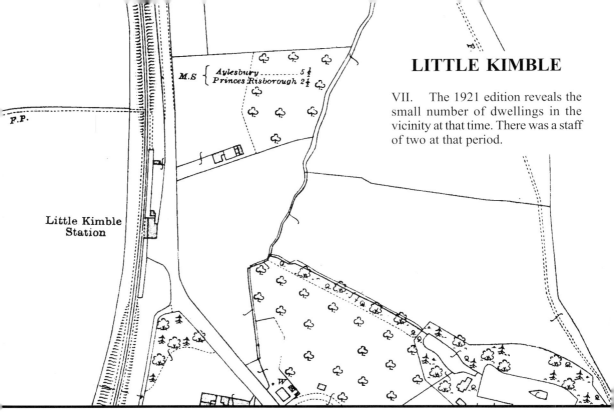

LITTLE KIMBLE

VII. The 1921 edition reveals the small number of dwellings in the vicinity at that time. There was a staff of two at that period.

15. The station first appeared in timetables in 1873. No. 1440 is propelling its autocoach back to Aylesbury on 2nd December 1961, by which time staffing had ceased but electric lighting had arrived. The population was 807. (B.Jennings)

16. Dieselisation brought more through trains to London and all ran direct, not via Maidenhead, after 1969. This is the 12.10 Aylesbury to Marylebone service on 19th December 1987, photographed during sign changeover. There were ten up trains at irregular intervals at this time. (P.G.Barnes)

17. The building became a private dwelling and the brickwork was pebble-dashed. No. 165023 approaches on 26th August 2002, forming the 13.17 from Marylebone. (M.J.Stretton)

MONKS RISBOROUGH

18. The halt opened on 11th November 1929 with the name as shown. The suffix was dropped on 6th May 1974, by which time the local population was over 1200.
(Lens of Sutton coll.)

19. The platform was shortened and a new hut provided, this having an unusual orientation. The revised arrangements are seen on 2nd December 1961 as no. 1440 departs with the 10.50am from Aylesbury. (B.Jennings)

20. A new platform was built about 150yds north of the original and was opened on 13th January 1986. It is seen on 9th October 1990 as an eight-car train calls on its way to Marylebone. It is the 10.51 from Aylesbury, but there were no passengers here. (M.J.Stretton)

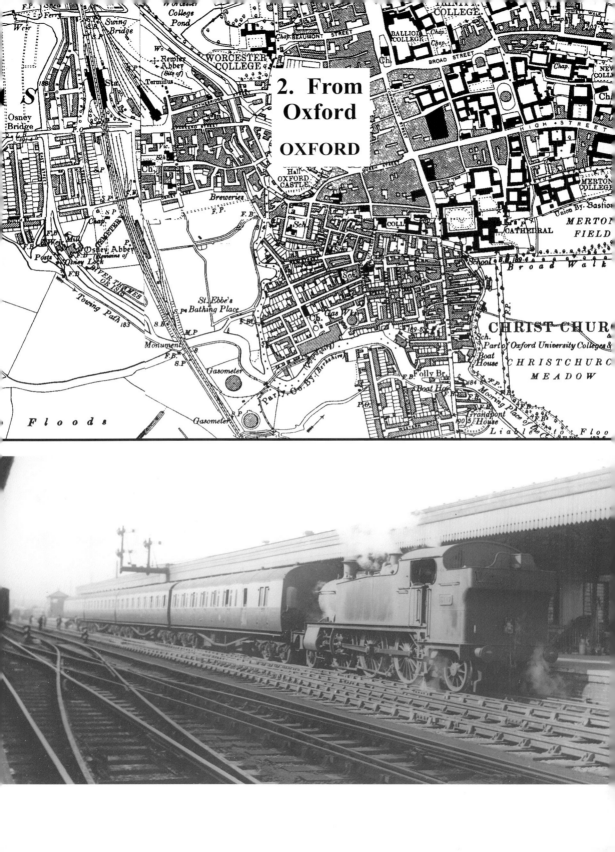

2. From Oxford

OXFORD

◀——— VIII. The first station was a terminus and was situated near the letters P.O. at the bottom of this 1900 map at 6ins to 1 mile. The nearby lines to the gasworks were in use between 1886 and 1967. Top left is the GWR station, with the LNWR terminus alongside. Below them is Becket Street Yard and below that is South End Yard.

◀——— 21. The through station opened in 1852 and the 1844 terminus closed to passengers that year, although it remained open for broad gauge freight trains until 1872. No. 5117 stands with a down train in 1938, when both platform lines had scissors crossovers with the through lines.
(Lens of Sutton)

22. The first station here had a roof over the tracks and the up side building was replaced by this one in 1890. This and the next photograph are from July 1953.
(Lens of Sutton coll.)

23. The down side was provided with an equally drab and plain structure, contrasting greatly with the city's fine architecture. A dismal and often congested subway connected the two sides. (Lens of Sutton coll.)

24. The GWR built the first generation of diesel railcars in the 1930s and by 1950 half the services through Thame were operated by cars of this type. No. W3W waits to depart for Princes Risborough at 2.40pm on 27th February 1954. (R.J.Buckley/Initial Photographics)

25. An animated view from 8th March 1961 includes two bay platforms and no. 5957 *Hutton Hall* passing through with freight. Second generation DMUs are at platforms 3 and 4. (M.A.N.Johnston)

26. No. 6150 takes water near the delapidated buildings on 18th August 1962, prior to departure for Thame and Princes Risborough at 4.54pm. The station was rebuilt in 1971 and again in 1990, when the city was at last given an impressive structure. (B.Jennings)

27. No. 44985 runs south on 21st July 1965 with a parcels train for Didcot, while a DMU hauls a bogie van towards the station. Quadruple track from here to Kennington Junction was completed in 1942 to increase capacity for wartime traffic. (E.Wilmshurst)

Other views of this station appear in
Branch Line to Fairford **and**
Didcot to Banbury, **the latter detailing the route south to Kennington Junction.**

ABINGDON ROAD HALT

28. Almost two miles south of Oxford station, the halt was open from 1st February 1908 until 22nd March 1915. Hinksey Halt was between the two and was in use in the same period, both being served by steam railmotors. This 1919 view reveals that one shelter had been removed by then. (LGRP/NRM)

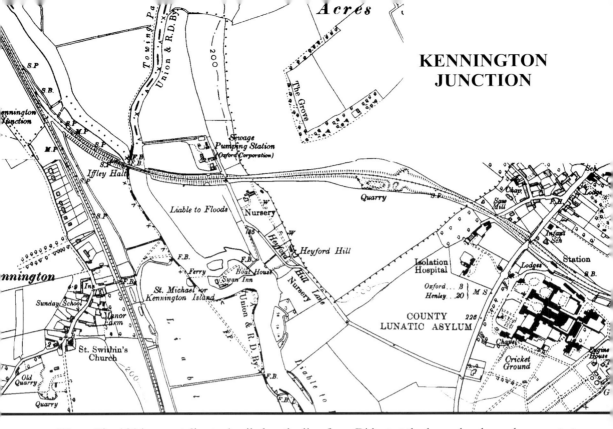

KENNINGTON JUNCTION

IX. The 1914 map at 6ins to 1 mile has the line from Didcot at the lower border and our route to Thame on the right. The locations of Iffley Halt and the station at Littlemore are shown.

29. The convergence of the two tracks towards Thame was recorded on 29th June 1963, along with the tablet catcher. On the left are the bowstring girders of the viaduct over the Thames. (P.J.Garland/R.S.Carpenter coll.)

30. Seen on the same day is no. 6154 leaving the single track, with examples of products of the Morris Cowley Works. The signalman will save himself the long walk to the tablet catcher. The signal box was in use from 1901 to 1973. The track behind the camera had been quadrupled in 1942.
(P.J.Garland/ R.S.Carpenter coll)

31. The fireman of no. 6111 is ready to surrender the single line tablet, as he approaches the junction in about 1966. The signals had been altered since picture 29 was taken.
(G.P.Cooper)

32. Kennington Viaduct suffered settlement and was completely rebuilt to the form shown in 1923. Part of the original abutment can be seen in this 1957 photograph. Iffley Halt was at the west end of the viaduct and was open for the period mentioned in caption 28.
(R.M.Casserley)

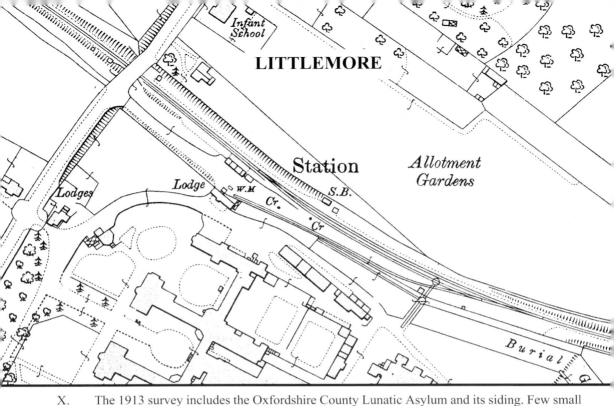

X.   The 1913 survey includes the Oxfordshire County Lunatic Asylum and its siding. Few small stations had two cranes. The traffic figures are shown overleaf.

33.   On the right of this 1919 panorama is the Littlemore Asylum, which had a private siding from a wagon turntable in the goods yard from 1870 until 1968. Its main purpose was coal conveyance. The signal box (left) had a 15-lever frame and was listed as a ground frame by 1938, but not at all in 1945. (LGRP/NRM)

34. A closer and later look at the station includes the goods crane which was rated at 3-ton capacity. Another and smaller winch is evident, this being provided for a pressurised oil lamp. The siding on the left served a fuel depot from 1929 and, after several periods of closure, reopened again in May 1997. (Lens of Sutton coll.)

35. No. 4103 was recorded in July 1959, by which time the dock siding was heavily overgrown, but it remained in place, along with the others, until 1972. Public goods traffic ceased on 21st June 1971. (H.Cowan)

Littlemore	1903	1913	1923	1933
Passenger tickets issued	13450	15545	4440	1585
Season tickets issued	*	*	5	1
Parcels forwarded	8311	12803	8199	6407
General goods forwarded (tons)	2784	5233	4542	1279
Coal and coke received (tons)	797	249	539	4485
Other minerals received (tons)	2910	4227	6104	5440
General goods received (tons)	3576	4266	7445	4163
Trucks of livestock handled	-	-	11	16

(* not available.)

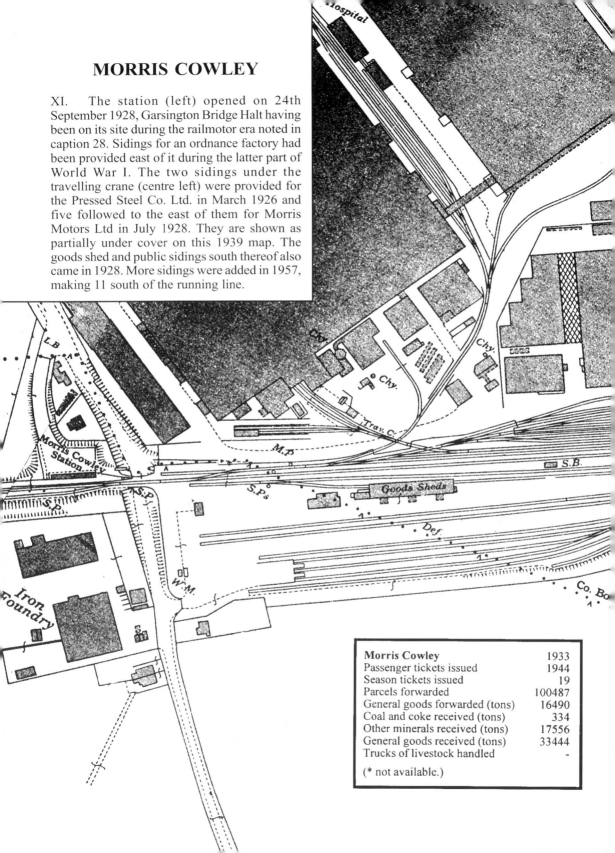

MORRIS COWLEY

XI. The station (left) opened on 24th September 1928, Garsington Bridge Halt having been on its site during the railmotor era noted in caption 28. Sidings for an ordnance factory had been provided east of it during the latter part of World War I. The two sidings under the travelling crane (centre left) were provided for the Pressed Steel Co. Ltd. in March 1926 and five followed to the east of them for Morris Motors Ltd in July 1928. They are shown as partially under cover on this 1939 map. The goods shed and public sidings south thereof also came in 1928. More sidings were added in 1957, making 11 south of the running line.

Morris Cowley	1933
Passenger tickets issued	1944
Season tickets issued	19
Parcels forwarded	100487
General goods forwarded (tons)	16490
Coal and coke received (tons)	334
Other minerals received (tons)	17556
General goods received (tons)	33444
Trucks of livestock handled	-

(* not available.)

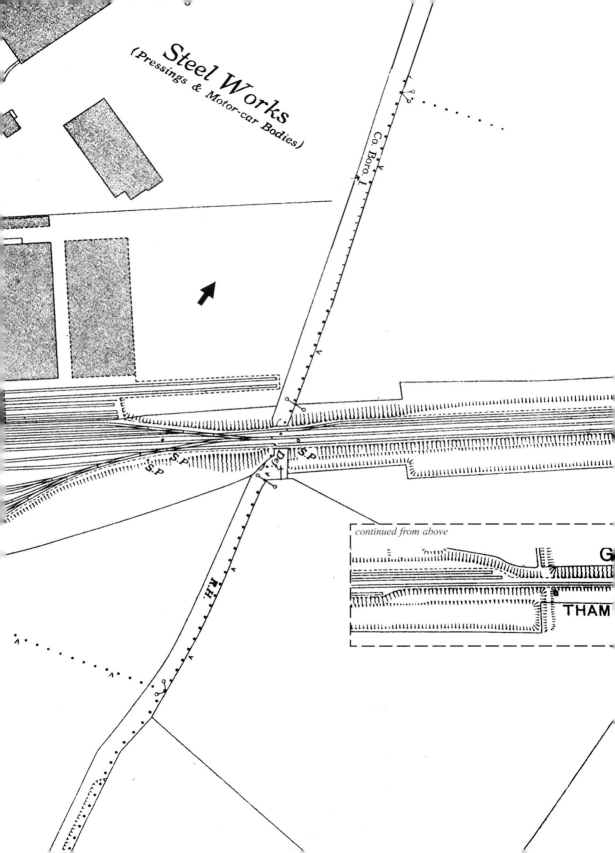

36. Lack of vegetation behind the platform suggests that this eastward view is from soon after the station opening. The 43-lever signal box, in the distance, was in use from 24th October 1928 until 28th January 1982. The 6.0am from Banbury terminated here with car workers and returned at 5.8pm (12.10pm on Saturdays) in the early years of the factory. (LGRP/NRM)

37. A train loaded with finished cars was recorded with no. 6340 on 14th November 1933. Many such trains ran to Brentford Dock with cars for export. (GWR/NRM)

38. The canopy was an afterthought and is seen in the 1950s. William Morris started repairing bicycles in 1892 and cars in 1901. Production of the "Bullnose" Morris Oxford began in 1913 and the Morris Cowley appeared in 1919. (Lens of Sutton coll.)

39. No. 6934 *Beachamwell Hall* was diverted from the Bicester route with the 4.10pm Paddington to Birkenhead on 11th September 1960. In the background is the motor factory which had also produced Wolseley cars since 1927. Riley Motors was acquired in 1938, when W.R.Morris became Lord Nuffield, a great benefactor of hospitals. A small one for his men is shown on the map. (M.Mensing/M.J.Stretton coll.)

40. No. 6124 was recorded with a train bound for Oxford on 14th April 1962, the British Motor Corporation having taken over the works (also Austin's) in 1958. The British Leyland Motor Corporation took control in 1968, but its bankruptcy in 1974 resulted in nationalisation. The Rover Group was formed in 1988 and many changes followed. (E.Wilmshurst)

41. BMW acquired the business in 1994, produced the last Rover in 2000 and concentrated on a new Mini. A new loading terminal was built and no. 60085 was named *MINI-Pride of Oxford* on 21st November 2001. Five double deck trains per week would each carry 264 cars to Purfleet in Essex for shipping to Zeebrugge, this amounting to 35% of production. (BMW)

HORSPATH HALT

42. The first halt was in use for the seven years given in caption 28. This is the second one, which opened on 5th June 1933 and was about 50yds west of the original. Both pictures are from the 1950s. (Lens of Sutton coll.)

43. Horspath Tunnel was nearly half a mile east of the halt and was 524yds in length. Its declining condition led to the closure of the route between Morris Cowley and Thame on 1st May 1967, the remaining freight operating over two separate branches. (R.M.Casserley)

WHEATLEY

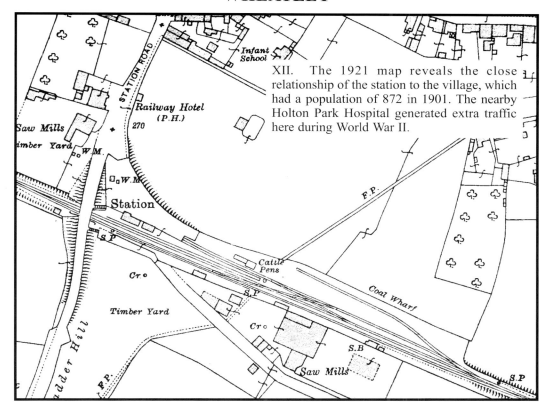

XII. The 1921 map reveals the close relationship of the station to the village, which had a population of 872 in 1901. The nearby Holton Park Hospital generated extra traffic here during World War II.

44. There was a staff of five for most of the 1930s, although it had been eight in the early years of the century. No. 1420 was recorded with a lightweight train from Oxford in July 1957. (H.Cowan)

45. A snap from the road bridge at about the same time shows the connection to the goods yard and a coke wagon to the left of the cattle pens. The line passes over the A40 in the distance, out of view. This bridge had to be lengthened in 1928 and again in 1961, when two spans were needed for dual carriageway. After a few years use, they were removed to serve elsewhere.
(Lens of Sutton coll.)

46. No footbridge was provided and so passengers could use the crossing in the foreground. No. 4147 is about to depart in August 1959, its four coach train filling the platform. (H.Cowan)

47. There were steps from both platforms to the bridge and so few would have used the crossing. The building with two chimneys in this 1962 photograph is thought to have been of Wycombe Railway origin. (E.Wilmshurst)

Wheatley	1903	1913	1923	1933
Passenger tickets issued	14777	19491	14940	6010
Season tickets issued	*	*	39	6
Parcels forwarded	36406	21562	19006	9072
General goods forwarded (tons)	2449	3172	2502	751
Coal and coke received (tons)	260	450	334	196
Other minerals received (tons)	2333	3340	3238	2096
General goods received (tons)	2319	2259	2336	1045
Trucks of livestock handled	259	181	258	179

(* not available.)

48. The goods yard handled only coal from 19th May 1964 until its total closure on 1st May 1967. The 25-lever signal box (right) was in use from 1892 until 12th July 1964, although passenger trains ceased on 7th January 1963. The crane was of six-ton capacity and is seen in June 1963. (P.J.Garland/R.S.Carpenter coll.)

Tiddington	1903	1913	1923	1933
Passenger tickets issued	10199	12189	7949	1871
Season tickets issued	*	*	25	3
Parcels forwarded	62983	33163	33724	9231
General goods forwarded (tons)	1175	1325	2243	262
Coal and coke received (tons)	72	15	194	84
Other minerals received (tons)	1420	3035	2539	568
General goods received (tons)	1141	1801	2323	779
Trucks of livestock handled	-	-	220	224

(* not available.)

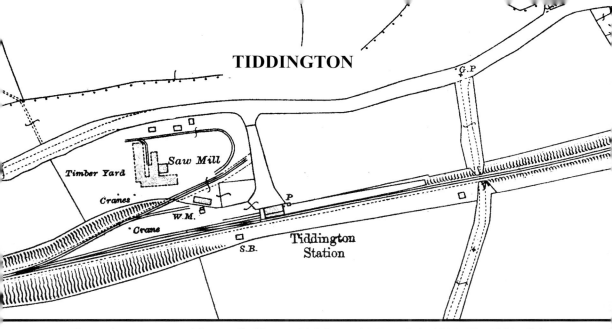

XIII. The station was west of the small village, which housed 168 souls in 1901. The 1921 edition includes a siding added for the Board of Trade timber supply depot.

49. This 1920 view includes many milk churns; agricultural produce and equipment were the main commodities despatched. There were four men employed here for most of the 1930s. (LGRP/NRM)

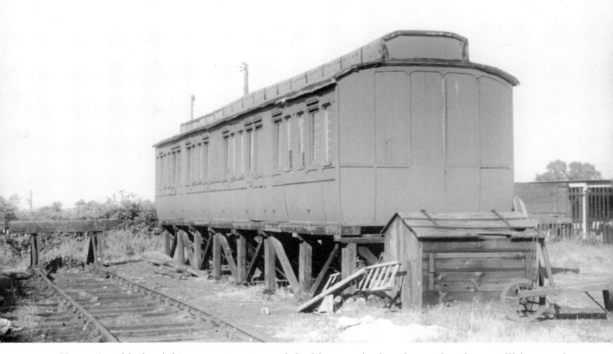

50. An elderly eight-compartment coach had been retired to the yard and was still intact when photographed in June 1957. It probably served the wood yard staff and arrived during World War I. (R.M.Casserley)

51. Relaying was in progress when the 11.5am from Princes Risborough called on 4th February 1962. The locomotive was 2-6-2T no. 6156. (B.Jennings)

52. Six months had elapsed since the last passenger used the platform and weeds were taking over. The siding remained usable until the end of 1963. (P.J.Garland/R.S.Carpenter coll.)

53. The signal box had been downgraded to a ground frame back in 1927 and was thus only used occasionally by the goods train guard when photographed in 1963. It had 15 levers in its frame. (P.J.Garland/R.S.Carpenter coll.)

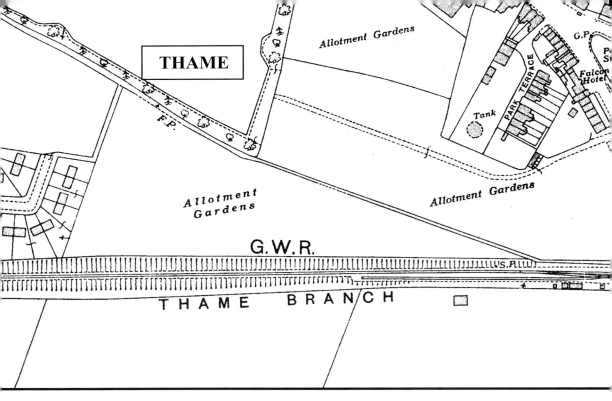

XIV. The 1937 survey is divided at the road bridge. The two long sidings north of the station had been added in the 1890s, otherwise little changed. The town grew from 2911 souls in 1901 to 4790 in 1961.

54. An early and indifferent postcard view from Chinnor Road gives a rare impression of commercial activity around 1900. There was a station staff of 15 recorded at this busy centre in 1903. A small crane is visible; by 1938, there was a six-ton one listed.
(Lens of Sutton coll.)

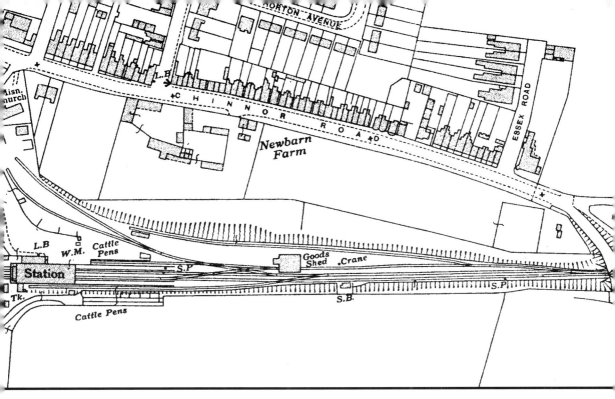

55. A 1920 picture features the Wycombe Railway's prestigious train shed which was based on one of Brunel's designs, but completed about three years after his death. Also included are the steps to the road and the pristine cattle pens. (LGRP/NRM)

56. The footbridge is not visible in the previous photograph, but its fine valencing can be enjoyed in this one. The water column for down trains is also evident in this view from the 1950s. (Lens of Sutton coll.)

57. In this panorama we have the tank that supplied the two columns and the station generally. The cattle pens on the left were added in 1931, but such traffic had increased only up to 1929 and then declined rapidly. (Lens of Sutton coll.)

58. No. 6124 is about to generate rhythmic echoes as it enters the mighty train shed, a smaller version of which still functions at the London end of the Wycombe Railway route at Maidenhead. The siding in the distance is one of three added in 1958 for an oil terminal. (M.J.Stretton coll.)

59. No. 6135 obstructs the barrow crossing as it waits to depart under superb strato-cumulus in July 1959. This angle enables us to examine the full length of the once busy yard. The two lamps indicated a train for London. (H.Cowan)

60. The cloud was thickening by the time that no. 1435 took water on the same day. A weighted point lever and a tapered wooden post will interest students of signalling history. Two local trains started their journeys here - the 12.11 and the 6.15pm - at that period. (H.Cowan)

Thame	1903	1913	1923	1933
Passenger tickets issued	28010	27921	26269	12353
Season tickets issued	*	*	77	94
Parcels forwarded	47648	60503	84308	52465
General goods forwarded (tons)	5624	5055	3714	1288
Coal and coke received (tons)	448	100	330	301
Other minerals received (tons)	4431	3626	6049	4005
General goods received (tons)	8860	6380	5076	2125
Trucks of livestock handled	683	1030	1313	431

(* not available.)

61. The 36-lever signal box was used from 1892 until 17th November 1968, but oil traffic continued until 12th April 1991, when a pipeline took over. The loop between the platforms remained in use to the end.
(P.J.Garland/R.S.Carpenter coll.)

62. The tanks of no. 6156 are being replenished while working the 10.0am service from Oxford on a Sunday in February 1962. A maroon coach follows one in red and cream; they remained so paired for some time on the route. (B.Jennings)

63. A short goods train waits in the dock while a DMU departs for Oxford on 14th April 1962. It will soon pass the oil terminal, beyond which the line was closed in 1967. The apron for washing out cattle wagons is also evident. The goods yard closed on 10th October 1966 and industrial premises were built on its site. (E.Wilmshurst)

TOWERSEY HALT

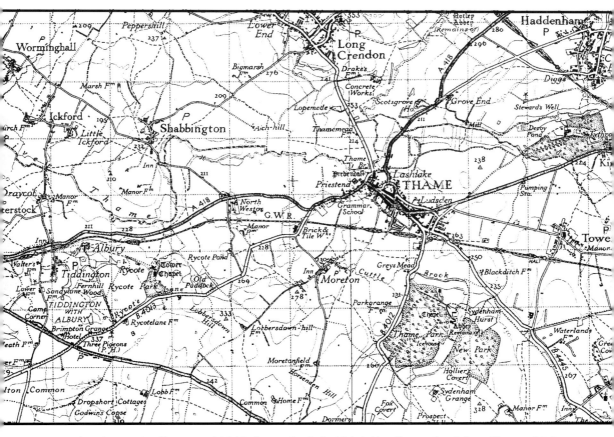

XV. The 1ins to 1 mile map of 1945 shows the halt (right) ½ mile south of the village, which housed 305 folk in 1901. The location of Tiddington is shown on the left.

64. The halt opened on 5th June 1933 and like other similar GWR structures, the name was shown on both sides of the board. (Lens of Sutton coll.)

65. A second view from the 1950s shows the oil lamps that were lit and extinguished by passenger train guards as required. (Lens of Sutton coll.)

66. No. 6149 was recorded with one of the two Sunday trains on 28th October 1962. It is the 10.0am from Oxford. After passenger services were withdrawn, some trains continued to run to the same schedule to carry parcels, causing fury locally. (B.Jennings)

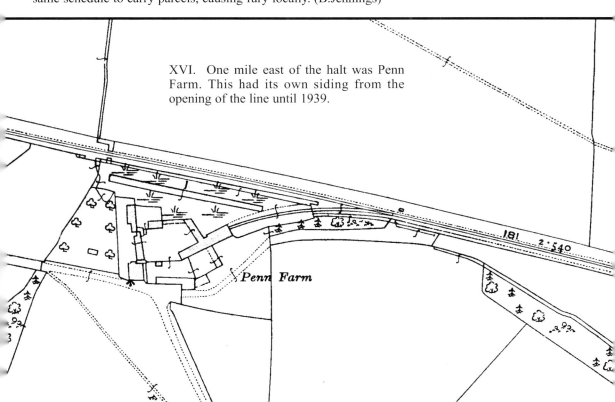

XVI. One mile east of the halt was Penn Farm. This had its own siding from the opening of the line until 1939.

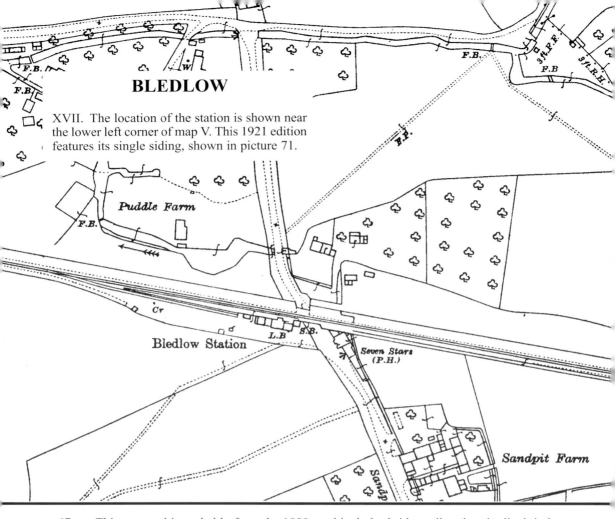

BLEDLOW

XVII. The location of the station is shown near the lower left corner of map V. This 1921 edition features its single siding, shown in picture 71.

67. This postcard is probably from the 1890s and includes bridge rail on longitudinal timbers, a system used by Brunel on broad gauge track. However, this has been narrowed by shortening the transoms. (Lens of Sutton coll.)

68. A 1919 view towards Oxford has the signal box steps on the left and the rods to the solitary point on the right. A staff of four was recorded between 1903 and 1938. Goods despatched included watercress and elm boles for trawling nets. (LGRP/NRM)

Bledlow	1903	1913	1923	1933
Passenger tickets issued	6121	4780	6488	5338
Season tickets issued	*	14	36	8
Parcels forwarded	5978	7427	9424	6529
General goods forwarded (tons)	612	859	448	2853
Coal and coke received (tons)	-	-	6	8
Other minerals received (tons)	106	389	456	137
General goods received (tons)	452	668	441	402
Trucks of livestock handled	-	-	-	-

(* not available.)

69. Looking in the other direction about 40 years later, we note only two significant changes - electric lighting has replaced oil and the waiting area has been panelled in. (Lens of Sutton coll.)

70. Seen in August 1959, no. 4147 is about to pass the signal box, which was in use from about 1892 to around 1938, when it became a ground frame simply controlling the gates. It had a 16-lever frame. (H.Cowan)

71.   Goods service ceased at the same time as those for passengers in January 1963 and the siding was lifted in 1964. Second generation DMUs worked some services in the final two years, such as the 12.21pm Thame to Paddington. (B.Jennings)

72.   Automatic half barriers were in use from September 1965 until line closure in 1991. The building (much extended) and some track were photographed in May 2002. (P.G.Barnes)

3. From Watlington

XVIII. This map is from 1947 and shows the remoteness of the terminus from habitation. A problem with land purchase prevented completion of the line to the town.

73. Although of poor quality, this view is included as it shows the engine shed which was destroyed by fire in 1906 and not rebuilt. A staff of four was recorded in 1903, this rising to eight from 1929 until 1933. (Lens of Sutton)

XIX. The 1921 survey gives the layout detail, which was almost unchanged throughout the life of the line. The WPRR kept its two Sharp Stewart locomotives here. One was a 2-2-2WT and the other a 2-4-0T. The latter is illustrated in picture 106 in *Branch Lines to Tiverton*.

Watlington	1903	1913	1923	1933
Passenger tickets issued	8363	24714	16183	11159
Season tickets issued	*	*	32	33
Parcels forwarded	19972	22773	22185	13395
General goods forwarded (tons)	2966	3300	2469	326
Coal and coke received (tons)	464	623	373	272
Other minerals received (tons)	1098	690	915	1121
General goods received (tons)	2471	2822	2050	1078
Trucks of livestock handled	43	41	54	18

(* not available.)

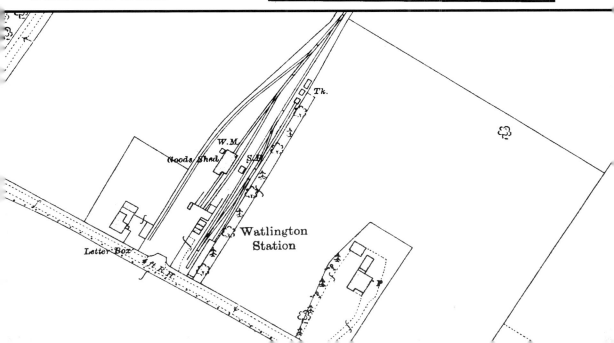

74. The carriage shed was at the other end of the site and was of the "Titfield Thunderbolt" pattern. As an economy measure, cattle used the same platform as passengers. The two small huts were oil stores and the tiny signal box was demoted to a ground frame in 1929, losing the signal seen in picture 73. (Lens of Sutton)

75. After arrival with the 1.54pm from Princes Risborough on 2nd November 1953, no. 3470 is reversing down the platform to take water. The coal wagon is marked LOCO; further coal stock is on the ground. The ladders and boards were used for coach cleaning on Sundays. (N.W.Sprinks)

76. Examples of low level platforms are to be seen in the following photographs of the halts. The autocoaches were provided with steps that could be retracted under the floor by the guard, using a long lever in the vestibule. (N.W.Sprinks)

77. No. 5766 waits with the 3.0pm departure on 12th June 1957. Autocoaches were never propelled on this branch, probably due to the severity of the gradients. Until the final years, a locomotive stood overnight here and two sets of crew were provided, with a fifth man on night duty. (R.M.Casserley)

78. The goods office and the water tank are clear in this picture of no. 4650 on 27th June 1957. In the last years of operation, an engine ran from Slough at 5.38am each morning to start the branch service here. Electric lighting had arrived in 1936. (A.E.Bennett)

79. A small crowd gathered on the last day of passenger operation, 29th June 1957. A bicycle, a motor scooter and a Morris 8 offered alternative forms of transport. Note that a bicycle shed had been provided and that the booking office had hinged shutters. (R.M.Casserley)

80. A special train organised by the LCGB brought a crowd on 3rd April 1960, nine months before total closure. It was part of the "Six Counties Tour" hauled mostly by *Evening Star*. The buildings lasted until 1963. (A.E.Bennett)

81. The last scheduled freight departed at 11.10am on Friday 30th December 1960 and comprised three empty wagons behind no. 41272, the 7000th locomotive from Crewe Works. The contents of the office were conveyed in the brake van on this cold, wet and miserable morning. (B.Jennings)

82. By April 1961, nature was taking over, but lights remained on three posts. These had served the lone engineman who cared for a solitary engine over a pit in the single shed-less siding each night. A grounded horse box was his shelter until 1951, when it vanished in smoke. (P.J.Kelley)

LEWKNOR BRIDGE HALT

83. The halt came into use on 1st September 1906 and was accessed by two flights of steps from the road below the bridge, which was photographed in 1919. (LGRP/NRM)

84. A 1956 view towards Chinnor includes evidence of maintenance work, but there were few to appreciate it. The nearby small village had an adequate bus service with lower fares than BR. (E.Wilmshurst)

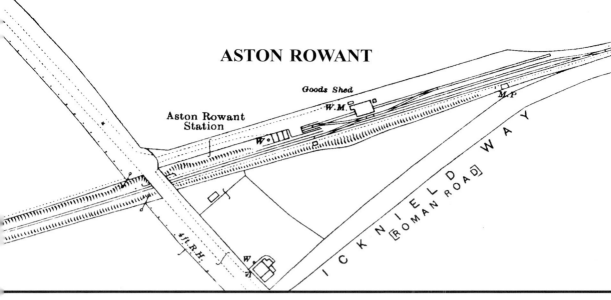

ASTON ROWANT

XX. The isolated station was provided with a well (W) and a weighing machine (W.M.) and is seen on the 1921 edition. The population of the village dropped from 579 in 1901 to 477 in 1961. The connection to the running line at the east end of the yard was made in 1929.

Aston Rowant	1903	1913	1923	1933
Passenger tickets issued	4352	2493	2600	708
Season tickets issued	*	*	11	2
Parcels forwarded	12641	9165	9392	2245
General goods forwarded (tons)	1433	1951	1637	358
Coal and coke received (tons)	293	265	88	119
Other minerals received (tons)	442	801	2041	1407
General goods received (tons)	365	1042	967	243
Trucks of livestock handled	7	13	37	7

(* not available.)

85. The Chilterns and the hay rick set the rural scene for this postcard panorama. Two men were employed here for most of the 1900-40 period. (Lens of Sutton coll.)

86. The porters would have had adequate time to tend the rambling roses and to use the handwheel (left) to raise water. The goods shed had a separate office and was equipped with a one-ton crane. (Lens of Sutton coll.)

87. No. 3697 brings a few moments of activity as it rumbles in from Watlington on 28th August 1954. The yard here was used in March 1963 for loading the lifted track components onto lorries. The A40 passes over the bridge. (N.Simmons)

88. Seen on the same day, this notice could have stated that there would be up trains at 8.52, 11.38 and 3.3 only and down ones at 10.40, 2.12 and 6.6. The 8.20pm mentioned ran on Fridays only. (N.Simmons)

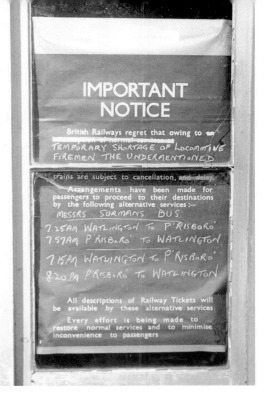

89. The architectural details were being admired on 20th September 1959 from the comfort of a MG Magnette. All three WPRR stations were built using flints from the Chilterns and had brick quoins. Demolition took place in the Spring of 1963. (B.Jennings)

90. The ground frame was unlocked by a key on the end of the single line token. The line was built cheaply by minimising earthworks, as is evident by the gradient in the distance. Model railway enthusiasts never need to worry again about undulating trackwork. (Lens of Sutton)

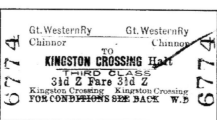

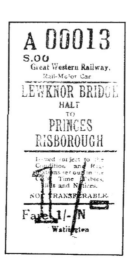

KINGSTON CROSSING HALT

91.   This halt came into use on 1st September 1906 and was photographed in 1919. The village of Kingston Blount was half a mile to the north. The signal wire ran to a distant signal. (LGRP/NRM)

92.   The proximity of the scarp edge of the Chiltern Hills is evident in this 1957 panorama. The track seems well cared for; high standards were usually maintained to the end. (R.M.Casserley)

CHINNOR

XXI. Elijah Benton of Acton started lime burning here in 1908 and was soon consuming 1200 tons of coal annually. Two years before this map was produced in 1921, he began producing cement and the GWR was bringing in 12,000 tons of coal and 2400 tons of gypsum by 1927. Most cement and lime left by rail at this time, but only half the output did so by 1940. By 1956, the coal tonnage was 62,500, much of it coming from Bolsover in Derbyshire. About 15,500 tons of gypsum came from East Leake, near Nottingham at this period. The total was about the same in 1979 and Chinnor Industries had become part of the Rugby Portland Cement Company. About 1550 tons of cement left by rail annually in the late 1960s, destined for Redland Pipes at Hamworthy in Dorset. Traffic ceased on 20th December 1989 and official closure was on 16th July 1990. The Chinnor & Princes Risborough Railway Association began collecting rolling stock in the cement works sidings with the aim of reopening the remaining part of the branch. Cement production has ceased.

Chinnor	1903	1913	1923	1933
Passenger tickets issued	6402	6116	8533	5533
Season tickets issued	*	*	17	48
Parcels forwarded	4841	6192	4070	5139
General goods forwarded (tons)	1434	1037	9628	5577
Coal and coke received (tons)	4	454	3192	539
Other minerals received (tons)	631	650	2801	2025
General goods received (tons)	1381	1061	1129	568
Trucks of livestock handled	-	53	24	4

(* not available.)

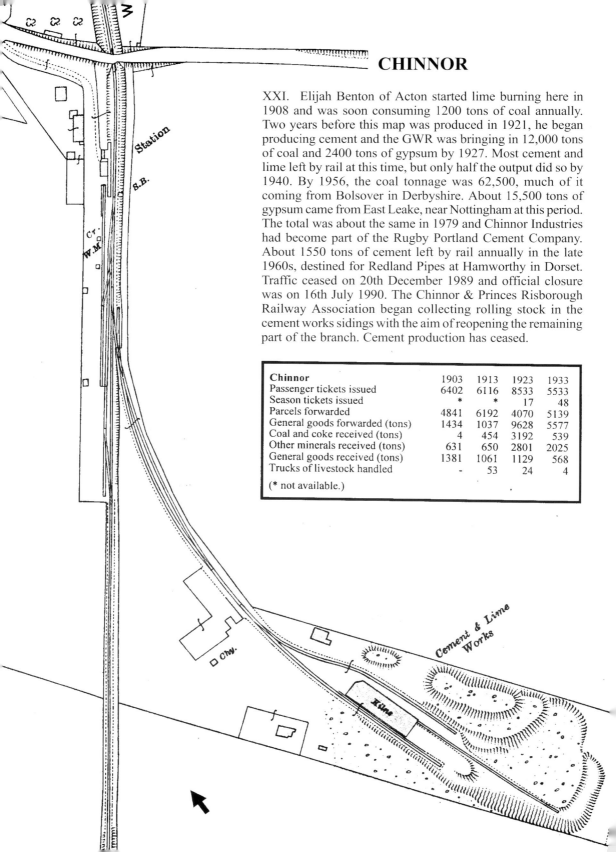

93. A postcard view towards Watlington shows more undulating track and that there was no connection to the running line at the far end of the goods yard. This was added in 1913. (Lens of Sutton coll.)

94. The ground frame hut and contemporary road transport are evident in this eastward record from around 1900. There was a staff of 4 or 5 in the subsequent 40 years or so. (Lens of Sutton)

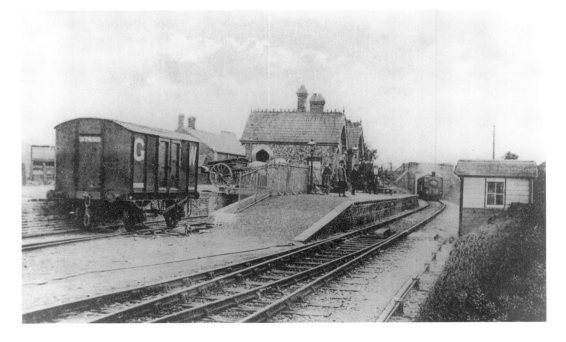

95. An August 1954 panorama includes the yard crane, which was rated at 1½ tons capacity, and the ground frame. After the arrival of a mineral train, the locomotive would run round and propel it into the private siding, where gravity would take over. (N.Simmons)

96. Looking east in 1957, we see the third and final WPRR station, together with a tank wagon. This contained water for engines shunting the cement works. In the foreground is a tramway that was laid across the road to a timber mill in 1949. (R.M.Casserley)

97. A June 1961 photograph shows the crane being used to load timber. The end of the branch was in the background from January of that year. (P.J.Garland/R.S.Carpenter coll.)

98. In the early 1960s, some BR 2-6-2Ts from Aylesbury shed worked the coal trains. However ex-GWR class 1600 and 3600 0-6-0PTs returned in 1962. The date of this photograph is 4th November 1961. The goods yard remained open for local traffic until 10th October 1966, by which time diesel locomotives had taken over. (B.Jennings)

99. Two class 33s are passing the site of the station with empty coal hoppers in the late 1980s. The loop is on the right. The works had five parallel lines at its optimum. (J.Treymaine coll.)

100. The CPRRA began a limited operation in 1994 from its base at Chinnor. The platform was lengthened to take four coaches and is seen on 7th May 1995 as 0-4-2T no. 1466 returns from the new run-round loop at Thame Junction. The locomotive was normally based at the Didcot Railway Centre. The railway carried over 15,000 passengers in 1996. (P.G.Barnes)

101. Work started in 1998 on the reconstruction of the station building, but a locomotive crisis arose and the tiny Barclay 0-4-0ST *John Howe* was obtained on loan from Carnforth. It is seen with two MkII coaches, its maximum load, on 16th August 1998. (D.Trevor Rowe)

102. Residents and a business use the original approach road and so car parking had to be on the south side of the line; a foot crossing was provided over it. The 15.15 is obscuring it on 12th May 2002. Haulage is by class 17 no. D8568. (P.G.Barnes)

103. Seen more clearly on the same day is the splendid replica station, correct in every detail. The ex-Cambrian Railway coach on the left had served as shop and cafe; it would function as the latter in future. Railcar no. W55023 was operating the service. Train times can be obtained by telephoning 01844 353535. (P.G.Barnes)

WAINHILL CROSSING HALT

104. The standard crossing keepers cottage is seen again, but the halt was built after the others, opening on 1st August 1925. The gates and halt have been restored by the CPRRA, but the house is privately owned. This eastward view is from 1957. (R.M.Casserley)

BLEDLOW BRIDGE HALT

105. This is the last of the halts provided in 1906 with the introduction of steam railmotors. These were not used on the branch for long. This is a 1957 view towards Watlington. The low level platform has been recreated by the CPRRA, although non-functional. The locality is known as Bledlow Ridge, not Bledlow Bridge. (E.Wilmshurst)

WEST OF PRINCES RISBOROUGH

106. A photograph from about 1951 shows the branch meeting the Thame route (left), almost one mile from the station. The two routes ran parallel for this distance, their separate distant signals being visible. (R.S.Carpenter)

107. The 3.5pm from Watlington is nearing the station on 14th March 1953, hauled by no. 4691. The signal for its line is of GWR origin, whereas those on the other post are upper quadrant LNER items, reflecting the joint nature of the lines through the station. They applied to trains from Thame. (N.W.Sprinks)

108. This is the location seen in picture 106, but is viewed in the opposite direction in May 2002. Termed "Thame Junction" by the CPRRA, it is the limit of operation from Chinnor, the line on the right being used by engines running round trains. (P.G.Barnes)

4. Princes Risborough

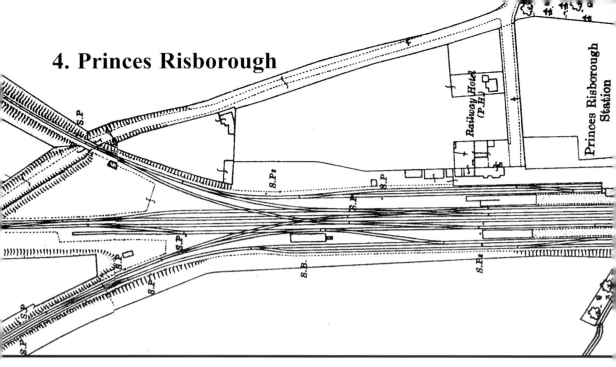

XXII. The 1921 edition has the single line to Aylesbury top left and the parallel single lines to Thame and to Watlington lower left. The goods yard is on the right page. There had been a separate platform on the left for Watlington trains until 1883. Note that these trains could only enter the bay platform, whereas those from Oxford had a choice.

109.   We start our visit to the station by looking at two through trains. This is the 11.25am Oxford to Paddington, which had graced the Thame route on 10th September 1952. The five non-corridor coaches were hauled by "Star" class 4-6-0 no. 4053 *Princess Alexandra*. The two through tracks and the graceful footbridge date from the rebuilding of 1905 associated with the doubling of the route to London.   (N.W.Sprinks)

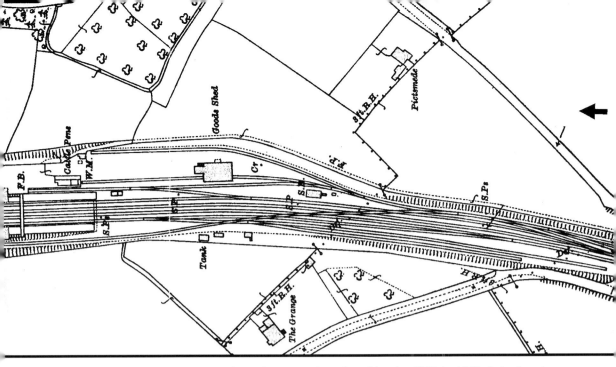

110. No. 65390 was an ex-LNER class J15, a type introduced by the GER in 1883. It is shunting a Watlington freight train on 31st July 1957 and is on the goods line, which ran passed the station on its west side. (H.Cowan)

111. No. 1442 runs in with three coaches and a horse box from Oxford on 14th March 1953. The locomotive is now in Tiverton Museum. North Box ceased to be so described when South Box closed in September 1966. (N.W.Sprinks)

112. No. 3694 sets off with the 6.50pm to Aylesbury on 6th May 1953, while the 6.58 to High Wycombe stands at the up platform. It had left Aylesbury at 6.25. There was another bay at the far end of the platform until 1968. (N.W.Sprinks)

113. The Aylesbury branch train has been brought in by no. 6429 on the 4th June 1960 to almost touch a van in the up bay. In the distance is the goods yard, which closed on 10th October 1966. (H.C.Casserley)

114. The Aylesbury shuttle was being worked by 0-4-2T no. 1453 on 14th April 1962. The Railway Hotel (right) is thought to date from the opening of the Wycombe Railway, but it was destroyed by fire in 1962. (E.Wilmshurst)

115. A four-car DMU has arrived from London at 6.41pm on 5th June 1962 and is running forward prior to reversal to the down platform and departure to Marylebone. Its Oxford connection (right) is ready to leave at 6.48 and the Aylesbury service (left) is due to go at 6.50. (B.Jennings)

116. The 1.20pm from Oxford has arrived behind no. 6124 on 8th September 1962. The engine will be uncoupled and will soon run over the crossover in the centre of the picture. This connects to the "Back Line", the goods loop seen in photographs 110 and 115. The Watlington branch brake van is parked on the siding to Forest Products, which was in use from 1927 to 1971. The milepost shows the distance from Northolt Junction. (B.Jennings)

117. The panel in the background was added in 1968 to control the line to Bicester North. The number of levers then dropped from 125 to 57 and track simplification resulted in only one bay and one through platform being in use. The box closed on 6th March 1991, since which time the area has been controlled from Marylebone. (B.W.Leslie)

118. Some stock from the CPRRA appeared at the disused down platform on 25th April 1992, as part of the event mentioned in caption 11. The locomotive was Sentinel no. 6515 of 1926 and it stands on the line leading to engineers sidings. The former down through line was still in use. (S.P.Derek)

119. A class 165 DMU leaves the Aylesbury branch to join the up main line on 11th March 2002. The former line to Thame curves left and links to a track behind the listed Grade II signal box to connect with the three engineers sidings. This arrangement severed the connection with the Chinnor line in 1998. (M.Turvey)

120. The track on which the train is standing in picture 118 was removed to allow the construction of a new down platform, this opening on 1st March 1999. It can be used by up trains terminating here, but the up platform is signalled for full reversible running. It is hoped that steam trains from Chinnor will have their own platform here one day and be signalled from the mighty box once more. (P.G.Barnes)

Details of the main line changes and other pictures of this station can be found in *Paddington to Princes Risborough* and *Princes Risborough to Banbury*.

Easebourne Lane, Midhurst, W Sussex. GU29 9AZ Tel: 01730 813169 Fax: 01730 812601
Email: enquiries@middletonpress.fsnet.co.uk *If books are not available from your local transport stockist, order direct with cheque, Visa or Mastercard, post free UK.*

BRANCH LINES
Branch Line to Allhallows
Branch Line to Alton
Branch Lines around Ascot
Branch Line to Ashburton
Branch Lines around Bodmin
Branch Line to Bude
Branch Lines around Canterbury
Branch Lines around Chard & Yeovil
Branch Line to Cheddar
Branch Lines around Cromer
Branch Lines to East Grinstead
Branch Lines of East London
Branch Lines to Effingham Junction
Branch Lines around Exmouth
Branch Lines to Falmouth, Helston & St. Ives
Branch Line to Fairford
Branch Lines around Gosport
Branch Line to Hayling
Branch Lines to Henley, Windsor & Marlow
Branch Line to Hawkhurst
Branch Lines around Huntingdon
Branch Line to Ilfracombe
Branch Line to Kingsbridge
Branch Line to Kingswear
Branch Line to Lambourn
Branch Lines to Launceston & Princetown
Branch Lines to Longmoor
Branch Line to Looe
Branch Line to Lyme Regis
Branch Lines around Midhurst
Branch Line to Minehead
Branch Line to Moretonhampstead
Branch Lines to Newport (IOW)
Branch Lines to Newquay
Branch Lines around North Woolwich
Branch Line to Padstow
Branch Lines around Plymouth
Branch Lines to Princes Risborough
Branch Lines to Seaton and Sidmouth
Branch Lines around Sheerness
Branch Line to Shrewsbury
Branch Line to Swanage *updated*
Branch Line to Tenterden
Branch Lines around Tiverton
Branch Lines to Torrington
Branch Line to Upwell
Branch Lines of West London
Branch Lines around Weymouth
Branch Lines around Wimborne
Branch Lines around Wisbech

NARROW GAUGE
Branch Line to Lynton
Branch Lines around Portmadoc 1923-46
Branch Lines around Porthmadog 1954-94
Branch Line to Southwold
Douglas to Port Erin
Douglas to Peel
Kent Narrow Gauge
Northern France Narrow Gauge
Romneyrail
Southern France Narrow Gauge
Sussex Narrow Gauge
Surrey Narrow Gauge
Swiss Narrow Gauge
Two-Foot Gauge Survivors
Vivarais Narrow Gauge

SOUTH COAST RAILWAYS
Ashford to Dover
Bournemouth to Weymouth
Brighton to Worthing
Eastbourne to Hastings
Hastings to Ashford
Portsmouth to Southampton
Ryde to Ventnor
Southampton to Bournemouth

SOUTHERN MAIN LINES
Basingstoke to Salisbury
Bromley South to Rochester
Crawley to Littlehampton
Dartford to Sittingbourne
East Croydon to Three Bridges
Epsom to Horsham
Exeter to Barnstaple
Exeter to Tavistock
Faversham to Dover
London Bridge to East Croydon
Orpington to Tonbridge
Tonbridge to Hastings
Salisbury to Yeovil
Sittingbourne to Ramsgate
Swanley to Ashford
Tavistock to Plymouth
Three Bridges to Brighton
Victoria to Bromley South
Victoria to East Croydon
Waterloo to Windsor
Waterloo to Woking
Woking to Portsmouth
Woking to Southampton
Yeovil to Exeter

EASTERN MAIN LINES
Barking to Southend
Ely to Kings Lynn
Ely to Norwich
Fenchurch Street to Barking
Ilford to Shenfield
Ipswich to Saxmundham
Liverpool Street to Ilford
Saxmundham to Yarmouth
Tilbury Loop

WESTERN MAIN LINES
Bristol to Taunton
Didcot to Banbury
Didcot to Swindon
Ealing to Slough
Exeter to Newton Abbot
Newton Abbot to Plymouth
Newbury to Westbury
Paddington to Ealing
Paddington to Princes Risborough
Plymouth to St. Austell
Princes Risborough to Banbury
Reading to Didcot
Slough to Newbury
St. Austell to Penzance
Swindon to Bristol
Taunton to Exeter
Westbury to Taunton

MIDLAND MAIN LINES
Euston to Harrow & Wealdstone
St. Pancras to St. Albans

COUNTRY RAILWAY ROUTES
Abergavenny to Merthyr
Andover to Southampton
Bath to Evercreech Junction
Bath Green Park to Bristol
Burnham to Evercreech Junction
Cheltenham to Andover
Croydon to East Grinstead
Didcot to Winchester
East Kent Light Railway
Fareham to Salisbury
Guildford to Redhill
Reading to Basingstoke
Reading to Guildford
Redhill to Ashford
Salisbury to Westbury
Stratford upon Avon to Cheltenham
Strood to Paddock Wood
Taunton to Barnstaple
Wenford Bridge to Fowey
Westbury to Bath
Woking to Alton
Yeovil to Dorchester

GREAT RAILWAY ERAS
Ashford from Steam to Eurostar
Clapham Junction 50 years of change
Festiniog in the Fifties
Festiniog in the Sixties
Festiniog 50 years of enterprise
Isle of Wight Lines 50 years of change
Railways to Victory 1944-46
Return to Blaenau 1970-82
SECR Centenary album
Talyllyn 50 years of change
Yeovil 50 years of change

LONDON SUBURBAN RAILWAYS
Caterham and Tattenham Corner
Charing Cross to Dartford
Clapham Jn. to Beckenham Jn.
Crystal Palace (HL) & Catford Loop
East London Line
Finsbury Park to Alexandra Palace
Holbourn Viaduct to Lewisham
Kingston and Hounslow Loops
Lewisham to Dartford
Lines around Wimbledon
Liverpool Street to Chingford
London Bridge to Addiscombe
Mitcham Junction Lines
North London Line
South London Line
West Croydon to Epsom
West London Line
Willesden Junction to Richmond
Wimbledon to Beckenham
Wimbledon to Epsom

STEAMING THROUGH
Steaming through Cornwall
Steaming through the Isle of Wight
Steaming through Kent
Steaming through West Hants

TRAMWAY CLASSICS
Aldgate & Stepney Tramways
Barnet & Finchley Tramways
Bath Tramways
Brighton's Tramways
Bristol's Tramways
Burton & Ashby Tramways
Camberwell & W.Norwood Tramways
Clapham & Streatham Tramways
Croydon's Tramways
Dover's Tramways
East Ham & West Ham Tramways
Edgware and Willesden Tramways
Eltham & Woolwich Tramways
Embankment & Waterloo Tramways
Enfield & Wood Green Tramways
Exeter & Taunton Tramways
Greenwich & Dartford Tramways
Hammersmith & Hounslow Tramways
Hampstead & Highgate Tramways
Hastings Tramways
Holborn & Finsbury Tramways
Ilford & Barking Tramways
Kingston & Wimbledon Tramways
Lewisham & Catford Tramways
Liverpool Tramways 1. Eastern Routes
Liverpool Tramways 2. Southern Routes
Liverpool Tramways 3. Northern Routes
Maidstone & Chatham Tramways
Margate to Ramsgate
North Kent Tramways
Norwich Tramways
Reading Tramways
Seaton & Eastbourne Tramways
Shepherds Bush & Uxbridge Tramways
Southend-on-sea Tramways
Southwark & Deptford Tramways
Stamford Hill Tramways
Twickenham & Kingston Tramways
Victoria & Lambeth Tramways
Waltham Cross & Edmonton Tramways
Walthamstow & Leyton Tramways
Wandsworth & Battersea Tramways

TROLLEYBUS CLASSICS
Croydon Trolleybuses
Derby Trolleybuses
Hastings Trolleybuses
Huddersfield Trolleybuses
Maidstone Trolleybuses
Portsmouth Trolleybuses
Woolwich & Dartford Trolleybuses

WATERWAY ALBUMS
Kent and East Sussex Waterways
London to Portsmouth Waterway
West Sussex Waterways

MILITARY BOOKS
Battle over Portsmouth
Battle over Sussex 1940
Bombers over Sussex 1943-45
Bognor at War
Military Defence of West Sussex
Military Signals from the South Coast
Secret Sussex Resistance
Surrey Home Guard

OTHER RAILWAY BOOKS
Index to all Middleton Press stations
Industrial Railways of the South-East
South Eastern & Chatham Railways
London Chatham & Dover Railway
London Termini - Past and Proposed
War on the Line (SR 1939-45)

BIOGRAPHY
Garraway Father & Son